**W9-CEL-636**

Childen's
394.210
Dash

$28.50

DATE DUE			

PROPERTY OF
BEEBE LIBRARY
345 MAIN STREET
WAKEFIELD, MA 01880

DEC -- 2017

Columbus Day

by Meredith Dash

ABDO
NATIONAL HOLIDAYS
Kids

www.abdopublishing.com

Published by Abdo Kids, a division of ABDO, PO Box 398166, Minneapolis, Minnesota 55439.

Copyright © 2015 by Abdo Consulting Group, Inc. International copyrights reserved in all countries. No part of this book may be reproduced in any form without written permission from the publisher.

Printed in the United States of America, North Mankato, Minnesota.

052014

092014

THIS BOOK CONTAINS RECYCLED MATERIALS

Photo Credits: Getty Images, iStock, Shutterstock, Thinkstock, © a katz p.21 / Shutterstock.com

Production Contributors: Teddy Borth, Jennie Forsberg, Grace Hansen

Design Contributors: Candice Keimig, Laura Rask, Dorothy Toth

Library of Congress Control Number: 2013952104

Cataloging-in-Publication Data

Dash, Meredith.

Columbus Day / Meredith Dash.

p. cm. -- (National holidays)

ISBN 978-1-62970-043-4 (lib. bdg.)

Includes bibliographical references and index.

1. Columbus Day--Juvenile literature. 2. Columbus, Christopher--Juvenile literature. 3. America--Discovery and exploration--Spanish--Juvenile literature.   I. Title.

394.264--dc23

2013952104

Table of Contents

Columbus Day

We celebrate Christopher

Columbus on Columbus Day.

History

Christopher Columbus was born in Italy. He was an **explorer**.

Queen Isabella was the ruler of Spain. She had a job for Columbus. It was to find a new **route** to China and India.

9

Columbus left on August 3, 1492. Three ships set sail. They were the Niña, Pinta, and Santa María.

Columbus did not find China or India. On October 12, 1492, he found America.

13

The first Columbus Day was celebrated in 1792. It was the 300th **anniversary** of Columbus coming to America.

15

In 1937, Columbus Day became a national holiday. President Franklin D. Roosevelt signed it into law.

17

We celebrate Columbus Day
to remember Columbus' arrival
to America. Many **Europeans**
came to America after Columbus.

19

Today's Columbus Day

We celebrate Columbus Day every second Monday in October. New York City has a big parade!

More Facts

- Columbus made four voyages to America.

- The Santa María was wrecked in a coral reef off the coast of present-day Haiti.

- Niña and Pinta were actually nicknames. We know this because ships were always named after saints as a Spanish tradition.

Glossary

anniversary – a celebration of something or someone on the same day each year.

Europeans – people from Europe. Italians, the English, and the Irish are all people from Europe.

explorer – a person who investigates unknown regions.

route – a way or road for travel.

Index

abdokids.com

Use this code to log on to abdokids.com and access crafts, games, videos and more!

Abdo Kids Code:
NCK0434